I'll Buy You a Bird Instead

Natalie Easton

Copyright © 2022 Natalie Easton

All Rights Reserved. This book or any portion thereof may not be reproduced, in whole or in part, in any form (beyond that permitted by Sections 107 and 108 of the U.S Copyright Law and except by reviewers for the public press), without the express written permission of the publisher except for the use of brief quotations in a book review.

Easton, Natalie / author

I'll Buy You a Bird Instead / Natalie Easton

Poems

ISBN: 979-8-9869524-0-6

Edited by: Elisabeth Horan
Book Design: Amanda McLeod
Cover Art: Natalie Easton, created with NightCafe AI Generator
Cover Design: Natalie Easton and Amanda McLeod

PUBLISHER
Femme Salvé Books
An Imprint of Animal Heart Press
P.O. Box 322
Thetford Center, Vermont 05075
www.femmesalvebooks.net

Table of Contents

Scarlet I. Scarlet Fever	9
Scrapbook	10
Valentine	11
Anthem I. Driven	12
Jackie O.	13
Jack Nicholson is a Hypocrite	14
Anthem II. Everything Must Go	15
The Divorce: My Mother Becomes Real	16
Laws of Motion	17
Illinois I. The Bird Bribe	18
Illinois II. Empathy	21
Abstract	22
Aside: to the Grimm Grandmother	23
Scarlet II. Trading	24
Scarlet III. The Dishes Sit in the Sink	25
Things We Did After Your Death	27
Silver Bells	28
Scarlet IV. Thermography	30
Complicated Grief Reaction	31
Perspective	32
Anthem III. Return	33
Instead	35

Mom:

Scarlet I. Scarlet Fever

You laughed when I said I thought
you were a carrier of strep. How funny
for your ten-year-old to come home from school

and accuse you thoughtfully of this.
Over and over I went to the nurse
with my throat veined white like a cut strawberry.

Lying in her little bed with its pulled curtain,
I felt coated in a safe green pill, waiting
for you to come along and pick me up.

You tucked me in when I sparked a rash,
before I lit with fever. I became a metaphor
of myself—slept with my eyes open.

Sister crept in to press a hand against
my doll-bright cheek: concern or curiosity
I was not awake to see.

You roused me with questions about the year,
the president's name. You threatened me
to make me eat: you'd have them put

                        a needle in my vein.

Scrapbook

I was a little version of Mom to scale, scaled
right down to the lizard brain. Sister taught me
how to look: she looked away. We survived

the laughing father friendly enough to unpack
a Mack truck and make a friend: laughing father
needed enough to be reined in from long-haul

fucking to short-haul home-late. The crabs
came from a toilet seat, and coincidentally
he had moved a mattress that day.

His mantras were *Black boys* and *checkbook,*

—disrespect

if someone spoke of his saintly mother,
ghost-thighed, who oversaw the marriage

in a church basement. How to love oneself
within one's self-deprecation. & Sister in the back yard
on the swing with a boy. Sister pillow-thighed.

Sister in the vice principal's desk scouting liquor.
Sister missing & I prayed for her invisibility or mine.
Sister thrown against the wall, lollipop clutched

in one hand, the dimes not spent at the payphone
in the other; she was ready to laugh about this later.
Sister to a movie camera. Sister to a security camera.

Sister to a space telescope. Sister resented. Sister
hated. Sister illustrated on a leaf of my brain
in a book I've closed. First book I wrote. First book

                I'd save from a burning house.

Valentine

After Easter we'd mist our hair with lemon,
lounge in the sun beside Mom's garden
with its gray pearl slugs, its green spokes

razored together, thick as Velcro.
February's pink hearts dozed away, drawered
& sleeping on their sleeves.

And if a robin's egg fell on the lawn,
I recall it in the kitchen
scrambling breakfast this morning,

this year. My hands have turned to whisks
and I am omniscient, which means
I don't know which parts of the past

to throw away. My paper mailbox
overflows with cut expressions: our mother,
two years dead now, looks out the kitchen window

at us lazing on the lawn. We don't notice.
Go in, I will my former self.
Just for a glass of water.

Anthem I. Driven

Mom, you let your story drop
like a low note in a heavy song:
preparing your sisters' hair for school,

you learned to braid the way you would for me—
the brush held hard & angry, raking.

You had your first child young, & ran away.
                             A step up
to that golden boy slumming it.

Tender as you were to his Midas touch,
you were slow to catch fire & kindle me:

a torch-haired child
with a memory from your pregnancy
lodged like a wisdom tooth in my jaw

until I was seventeen. I spit it out in the car,
watched your eyes widen. You said

this like a plea: I
                 couldn't remember

Sister crossing the lawn in her Girl Scout dress.
You must have worried what else

I'd escaped you with, what part
of your history it was my job to repeat:

we both knew it wasn't my sibling
I'd come searching for—I'd slipped from you
too urgently, to take my first direction from

         the overwhelmed expression on your face.

Jackie O.

"They're just staring because we're beautiful,"
you'd say. After a while we figured

it must be your Jackie Onassis hair,
not your hand holding mine

'til age twelve, your pinky tucked
between our palms like a small animal

burrowing away from the light. I found it
comforting and irritating: your long nail

mindlessly chafing, hard as a beak.
We slipped under the lights, ducked our chins,

      did our famous grocery shopping.

Jack Nicholson is a Hypocrite

"What if this is as good as it gets?"
—Melvin Udall

Jack Nicholson sat down at the table, ordered a short stack
and told me how it was, laying out his plastic fork

vertically. "Look," he said, "your sister is a bitch."
She'd tease: *She's so dirty she can't eat the things she touches.*

He leaned over his plate, pointed his knife, and pulled the trigger
on a frightening wink. "Sometimes a duck is a duck, and

a bar of soap is just slippery." He was all talk. I knew
that if I touched him, he'd bolt to scrub his red hands clean.

I'd keep eying pepper suspiciously. And if something on my plate
seemed poison, I'd ask Mom to share it with me.

Anthem II. Everything Must Go

Summer ride, seats hot enough to paint our pale
white thighs with red welts, Moody Blues
playing loud—

we followed arrows on weathered signs:

Multi-Family - Rain or Shine - Moving Soon!!!

Sometimes we drove slowly by,
scanning lamps, old TVs.
I learned your taste for the unique:

fifty cents for the shorts someone else cut
from a pair of jeans

      (you'd stitch
      on a
      beaded fringe).

& the hours the cart spent
threading through department stores,
sewing up your restlessness;
my mouth stayed good and obedient—

I tried to revoke Sister's name-brand tongue
with my restraint.

You broke my heart by wanting things,
                then putting them away.

The Divorce: My Mother Becomes Real

Among kicked beer cans, your pills
have gone missing.
You ache with expectation:

    what will the husband do?

You're the woman
from the bathroom floor
with serotonin syndrome
again, cleaning dirt from the linoleum
with steak knives;

    an ambulance arrives

while your teenage daughter
reads an old book in her room.

You rise
from a sea of perfectly cooked
scallops with butter, a golden myth
of housewives.

    Handcuffs are produced.

You darken into the night—
glint like a black sky scuffed white
with stars, or like the button eye
of an old, faithful toy once held close

    during a long, delirious illness.

Laws of Motion

Hunting season you'd slow down & honk
to a bevy of flipped white tails, angry

flashes of orange. That's how the memory
begins, as if it started there: a small town

cliché. Your boyfriend went crazy, pulled
a gun on us one night—I remember

the bullets on top of the fridge, how your cat
went missing. Other than that it's scattered,

like our police reports. My wet nose &
oil-gloss eyes in the neighbor's kitchen;

I was a doe, all limbs & prickly hair.
At the head of the drive, in the flashing lights,

I moved in; you pushed me back. For every
action, an equal & opposite—that much

still makes sense. There are those who
let things go: kids with balloons, to see how far

they'll fly; Buddhas & saints; the dying before
they leave. I am not these—I remember:

his gun, the beam of his flashlight, the sound
of the door you slammed to save me. & then

the recurring dreams: I could not find my class.
I woke to become the homeless girl thumbing

ten dollars in the cereal aisle,
   going to school to drop Spanish III.

Illinois I. The Bird Bribe

"I'll tell you in another life, when we are both cats."
                              —Sofía Serrano

I.

New York never moved: in the gray light
it felt like we were entering the Earth's giant sadness,
and had to continue.

From the driver's seat
your lover's son tried to speak with me,
but I pulled my hat down over my two-tone hair
and thought about bleach.

Unflinching silence
was my forte. I thought the same of grief:
that some people are born to it
the way they are to disfiguring birthmarks:
a tea or strawberry stain across the skin,

              for no reason—

or even that tragedy finds the emptiness in people
as a way to bring them validity.
I slouched down in my seat; I couldn't sleep.

II.

We arrived to a view of the Mississippi,
and a graveyard of granite heads
bowed outside my window.
Mausoleums faced me, mocked my furnishings.

You lured me out with birthday cake
and a holiday: Cinco de Mayo
burned my throat, used the death wish to file my bones
with the saw of ten drinks,
                            but wouldn't release me.

I kept waiting to see what would happen—
I fell in love with this movie:

                        at the end
we find out the main character is cryogenically frozen;
he's been dreaming a painted life spiraled into dread,
and the faces of the ones he loves and hates
keep interchanging
until he remembers that he's dead—
had committed suicide to stop from aging
so he could cancel his inevitable future
and come back to a better place.
        Then he jumps off a building—

this was after the buildings fell. I'd watched
and wondered if my ex was in Manhattan.
I felt so ill
I wandered lost between the numbers
and the presidents, the states and the trees:
all those intersecting Midwestern streets.

III.

Every gaze seemed
to burn my skin raw.
I finally begged you to help me. Obscurely,
you took me out to shop;

that's when I saw the red parrot turn its head,
and I filled—like an urn—
with its beauty.

Later, when the invitation came to move to Pittsburgh
with a friend, you didn't ask me not to leave,
but the child in your eyes seemed to mourn and you said
that if I stayed, you would go out,

and you'd buy me the bird
                                    instead.

Illinois II. Empathy

The hardest thing for me to accept
about the bird we had struck

      was what you said

as we buried him under the garden bush:

      hunger had driven him to swoop to the asphalt
      for something he'd seen.

So that's what I thought of
years later
when I saw your plain white bowl
abandoned on the table top.

Eventually someone turned the dish over the trash,
washed the oily ceramic, put it on the drying rack;
it wasn't you. You were

  tired of being broke

but wouldn't say how much you took.

      If you weren't conscious in an hour,
      then I should make a call.

You came to my room to tell me this,
then went downstairs to cook.
Spaghetti with garlic.

Abstract

I.

And the expression when you saw me—
tired girl at the birthday party
accepting one last gift from the latecomer.
Then your one-armed hug—

and we settled in to wait
only
you didn't seem to know
what we were waiting for.

II.

Don't worry, they said.
She isn't hungry;
her body is consumed with dying.

Aside: to the Grimm Grandmother

You were a legend: a fairytale witch, crooked and pinch-faced over the cradle of your oldest. When you cried on the phone to me, I imagined you: evil forest incarnate, face of bark bitter for the apples picked from your tree. I have the feeling it was just as surreal for you: with your granddaughter on the line, it could no longer be *the flu* (like you'd told people in your enchanted way). This was the real world. People could really die, and she was going to.

Scarlet II. Trading

Your hand on the hospital phone: you answered with
What? not with *Who?* as if the only question

you had left was not who called, but what else to relate:
what other diagnosis of your heart taking on water,

like your lung—*I'm not in a hospital, I'm in a goddamn
ship on the ocean.* The needle prodding, then a port—

for you were at a place for trading—plugged below
your collar-bone. You told me that strange things

were happening: the woman sharing your room died,
then returned the next day to take up her knitting.

I agreed it was upsetting. I said your family seemed
to want something, that my phone was always ringing;

Don't you let them get away with that, you said.
They were never *there for me.* But they arrived in shifts

to hold up time, the junkie's vein, and didn't mind
if what you could offer was clean, or hard to come by;

they came to watch you revolve slowly into knowing
and out again, like an answer revealed and then—

months passing. I heard this from home, two states away,
impatiently strategizing the best time to step in:

                    close, but not too near, to the end.

Scarlet III. The Dishes Sit in the Sink

I attempt to hide your Lorazepam in apple sauce
while your cat prowls beneath the coffee table,

pees on the last thing you bought—embroidery floss—
for some unknown project, I think for me.

She hates everyone but you, has always known
it is a choice between you and everything else.

You once said you wanted her put down after;
no one else would love her—leaving her would be cruel.

If it's company you want, I'll voice my willingness.
Do you know that seeing the world your way

was the least I could do? I have tried to escape without
burying you. My last visit, the hospital called,

and these things went unsaid. The only question
I managed: who would do your housework when I left?

And that was how we cried—for the reality
of dish soap. Now I've returned to find that dying

creates a new formality: I say you've always looked
lovely in red, and you say thank you. Today you could

confuse me for a hospice nurse—one of the ones
who keep showing face—but they're just waitresses able

to bring something stronger than a cocktail (as long as
we can flag one down and get our order in). They

swab your mouth with pink toothettes, daily, on 15-minute shifts. They make me feel small by keeping you clean.

But we've always known that when it's time,
                              I'm the one who'll dose the morphine.

Things We Did After Your Death

I couldn't bear your naked body—the one that made you
cry as if for pleasure. In the moment I didn't know

my reasons why, only my discomfort. You peered at me
from the loose skin of starvation, like a girl flowing

from the folds of her mother's discarded dress.
You wanted the chair, so I claimed your hospital bed.

I lifted your weight despite my back and later never
felt the pain, but I couldn't wipe you after the bathroom,

or soap over the scar on your chest. In your illness
you were too new and innocent. I kept completely still

when your breath slowed to a lullaby pace; I couldn't
shake the idea that an irate stranger crawled

beneath the cradle, possessed of your memories.
But I knew you would say, "Don't let me go to the grave

dirty." So after you died, while my stepfather turned away
and wailed, I took a damp rag and wiped your lips.

However much beer that mouth drank, however many times
it humorously cussed, or said "I love you," however many

times it kissed a pet or chided a husband, it had closed
and was being touched for the final time by me.

For all I knew you felt it still, just as you heard me say
it was okay to take your last breath, and you agreed.

By this point the cat had disappeared,
and would not be seen for days.

Silver Bells

I.

You wouldn't let me place a gift for you
underneath the tree. In your final weeks,

you touched the wind chime in our favorite shop—
I didn't dare buy it for you. Later I went back

and claimed it for your friend. I wonder why
you wanted it; you knew you wouldn't see

your flowers open up beneath. By January
you'd known so long that your words burned

as they flew, like birds in a dream: how they drop
swift and unwanted, like ash on the mountain.

II.

It was not goodbye enough that you bit your lip
and showed me how to make your meatloaf.

I was waiting for a revelation—instead,
you fed me incessantly. You smoked.

That comforting sound, like a hot coal kissed.
All your things still smell of cigarettes.

In my dreams, you're always sick and angry.
In one, I bought you a fish tank; we waited

for the guppies to have babies. In another,
I planted you a garden whose every flower cast

its plastic gaze upon the sun. Not one time
in all these nights have you lit your glance on me.

But once, on a whim, I lifted the phone
before it rang, and your voice ran through

like you'd been waiting. "Don't be ridiculous,"
you gently scoffed.

                    "Of course we can still speak."

Scarlet IV. Thermography

Without any hesitation but the truth, I bare my breasts
for a woman I met five minutes ago. I bare them

for an intimate act that has more to do with who I am
on the inside than losing my virginity
to my first real boyfriend at sixteen and a half,

a ritual I made him wait almost two years for before
presenting myself without warning, a condom in one hand

and a course of synthetic hormones running
through my blood. She is about to see them: a map
of estrogen and consequence; a latticework of lingerie

underneath my skin. There is no protection this time,
just the fear that comes when my shirt slides back on

and I wonder again what I've done. When the results come,
they will not be suspicious, but not optimal, like the motives
of most who have touched me. The heat map will reveal

the yellow line of a vein branching across my right breast;
the terminology used to describe it will sound ominous.

The technician will reassure me, say I don't have anything
to worry about yet, that things can still be done to lower
my risk, but all I will hear in her tone is that

there is an equation inside me, and I will always need
someone else to tell me what it is.

Complicated Grief Reaction

The social worker dons a little commercialism
on the naked concept of her body, turns one shoulder
to me, and metaphorically winks like a shampoo ad.

She tells me she's looking forward to this, and
that's when I ask her if she'll take a check. When
the first tear falls, we'll pop a bottle of champagne.

If twenty minutes later I haven't ceased—
the ribbon-cutting ceremony. My new life
can open its doors onto the first room:

The Loss of the Mother. Statue daughters wait
headless, unable to cry. Their stone fingers are
poised in the open windows of their empty wombs.

They've been taught it can be healing to speak
to the dead, so this is what they do.
Every plaque reads, *I've written a letter to you,*

and this is where I'll keep it.

Perspective

Someday you'll want to talk to me, Natalie, and I won't be here.
                                    —Your journal, 2007

Months before your death, you began to withdraw.
Your phone was always off; you told me

bill collectors were searching for my step-brother.
It hurt to put your arms against your sides,

feel yourself breathing in the darkroom air.
The family shadows heated every occupied space,

hunted your possessions; your beagle watched you
from his chair. I was so proud of my desire

not to superimpose your life onto mine any longer—
to find that the lines met in a vanishing point—

I rarely tried to keep in touch. You felt it was time
to take the photos down; bears & wolves,

you told your husband, should replace
your children's faces on the wall.

Anthem III. Return

I never saw it coming—straight-faced,
you'd tell the cashier to check my ID,

or set Grandma up for something good:
"Hey Mom, does the president own Bush's Beans?"

When your father made the wrong remark
about cancer and your cigarettes, you quieted:

waited until he left to mention he'd bought
your first pack when you were thirteen.

If asked who you were I will say,
"The woman behind the wolf calendar—

the one crouched in my sense of humor
with a razor blade, a bottle of Valium,

and a crushing capacity for silence
cowering beneath the need to survive."

So I suggested that after you died
we'd take the ashes from the living room tray,

measure them out evenly, give them to your family,
and tell them that's how you'd burned

after smoking one butt too many. You laughed
so hard you coughed, your body like

a glowing spoon from which you'd not yet slid.
In that moment names could still be punchlines

to cover the hurt, and you were still a woman
who would fix a Thanksgiving plate

for your elderly neighbor when you saw
that no one else would visit him. And that,

I tell myself, is why it should all cease to matter:
the fact of no goodbye and no grave.

Now that I'm alone I know
       you'll never stop returning to me.

Instead

"When I'm gone I don't want you to sit around feeling sad over me."
—Final visit, February 2012

In black and white you pinch the pills, take them
in your thin dry mouth; fluid in color you lift
the blotter paper to your lips, lick a cartoon mouse.

The frames split clean: at the top of the set
you're fighting off the ambulance attendants,
being handcuffed and led away; on the bottom

you regard the girl next to you and see my face.
In '67 you are 17, not 6; your father can not
come home and lift his belt from the hook. Instead

you dance in California, color mandalas,
choose your lovers carefully. Time is a skin
you can see: a pregnant belly is a watch whose hand

moves in the middle of the night in a dark room.
And this is your life: the celebrities waiting
in their outrageous dress, film-ready. They could be dolls,

cardboard stand-ups, and should admit the joke
any minute: confess their strangeness, agree
to relinquish their costumes, step out and leave their bodies

standing behind like wax figures. Somehow the lens,
known for distortion—unflattering angles, an extra
ten pounds—refuses to ground them, to make them

pedestrian. As if your easy mind forgets the camera
dangling in your long ringless hand and takes the pictures
itself,

                                      everything opens up to you.

ACKNOWLEDGMENTS

These poems have appeared in the following publications, sometimes in earlier drafts:

Jet Fuel Review, April 2015: "Laws of Motion", "Perspective"

Rust + Moth, Spring 2014: "Scarlet IV. Things We Did After Your Death" (Pushcart Nomination), "Scrapbook"

Superstition Review, May 2015: "Trading"

Three drops from a cauldron, April 2015: "Aside: to the Grimm Grandmother"

Wild Goose Poetry Review, February 2013: "Scarlet IV. Thermography"

SPECIAL THANKS

The following programs and people made this book possible/improved it immensely with the generosity of their time and attention:

The Middlebury Bread Loaf Writers' Conference, Sally Keith, and everyone from my 2015 workshop group; Erin Elizabeth Smith of SAFTA/Firefly Farms; April Michelle Bratten, friend and editor of Up the Staircase Quarterly; friends and poets Laura Cherry, Kate Garrett, Jeremy Johnson, Ellyn Maybe, Rachel Nix, Russel Swensen, Raquel Thorne, and Angela Narciso Torres.

Finally I would like to thank my sixth-grade English teacher, Patricia Nilsson, who knew this book was forthcoming but who sadly passed before I was able to put it into her hands. Without her infinite warmth I would never have become a poet.

Advance Praise for *I'll Buy You a Bird Instead*

"Some of the trickiest relationships are often familial ones, and in Natalie Easton's *I'll Buy You a Bird Instead*, we confront this reality in heart-rending flashes of memory, through the lens of loss. While reaching an equilibrium between brutality and tenderness, Easton's poems take us by the hand to walk us through lives peppered with birds, cars, deer – existence in motion. We travel with the author across roads and phone lines, until we reach a stillness, an understanding with death. An important debut."

—Kate Garrett, author of *You've never seen a doomsday like it*

"In Natalie Easton's *I'll Buy You a Bird Instead*, she writes 'I thought ... of grief: / that some people are born to it,' and it would seem that our narrator is as she navigates an onslaught of loss, most notably her mother's death. In forthright and gutting language, this collection looks resolutely at the ways in which death and its preamble shape our existence in the world and the importance of how we communicate with our past in mourning. This is a beautiful book that will break your heart."

—Erin Elizabeth Smith, author of *DOWN*

"*I'll Buy You a Bird Instead* is a complex cry of longing – from a 'throat veined white like a cut strawberry' – for the ever-disappearing mother. These poems are painted in the many colors of illness, healing, resentment, surprising humor, regret: 'Go in, I will my former self. / Just for a glass of water.' From caring for the parent in extremis ('If you weren't conscious in an hour, / then I should make a call') to tending her body after death ('For all I knew you felt it still'), from denial ('I have tried to escape without / burying you') to acceptance ('Now that I'm alone I know / you'll never stop returning to me'), Easton brings a mother-daughter relationship – both foundational and impossible – into razor-edge focus, side-by-side with its loss. Easton's eye is unflinching, her portrayal of grief unstinting. The red bird glowing behind these poems – the parrot itself and the mother's devotion, even mixed with betrayal – is a reminder that love can wreck us and still we can be 'filled – like an urn – with its beauty.'"

—Laura Cherry, author of *Haunts* (Cooper Dillon Books)

"Devastatingly powerful, Natalie Easton's debut collection, *I'll Buy You a Bird Instead* sears deeply in the marrow."

—Ellyn Maybe, Poet/Musician/Lyricist

"If, as poet Marianne Boruch says, 'A poem is a box, to put other things in—for safekeeping,' then Easton's debut collection, *I'll Buy You a Bird Instead* is a series of nesting boxes, each more delicate than the last, each made to hold both the inscrutable pain of losing a mother and the vastness of her love, imperfect as that may be. 'I don't know which parts of the past / to throw away,' says the daughter, mourning her mother's slow fade into physical and mental illness. Yet these capacious, durable poems contain all that's worth keeping: 'your pinky tucked between our palms like a small animal / your long nail chafing…hard as a beak.' With lyrical fluency, narrative precision, and imagery sharp as cut gems, Easton teaches us how to look, how not to look away, and how to find what matters. 'Lodged like a wisdom tooth in [the] jaw,' these fierce and tender poems affirm that at the end of pain, what remains is wisdom. What remains is love."

—Angela Narciso Torres, author of *What Happens Is Neither*

www.ingramcontent.com/pod-product-compliance
Lightning Source LLC
Chambersburg PA
CBHW070454050426
42450CB00012B/3265